FEMALE FACETS:

Poems Celebrating Womanhood

Julie Anne Rudd

To Sarah,
Happy reading!
Best wishes,
Julie Anne
Rudd.

ACKNOWLEDGMENTS

With thanks to my husband, Chris, for affording me the time to indulge in my writing passion, to old friends Mel Peatfield and Delia Morley, who suggested I published my poetry collection, and to my proof-reader, Christine Fine.

FOREWORD

Somewhat later in life I have finally put together this collection of poems, scribbled down in notebooks over a number of years, as and when the mood has taken me. Mainly short, some longer, they reflect on everyday experiences on my journey through life. Some are light-hearted and amusing, some quirky, some tongue-in-cheek, while others are more serious, thought-provoking or written between the lines.

My passion for writing all started in school (my dear father, a writer himself, helping me to develop my inherited talent). Then, as a teenager, the flame of becoming a journalist was kindled and continued to burn brightly for me for some 30 years. I worked as a provincial newspaper reporter, enjoying the discipline of succinct writing, and later as a sub-editor, loving the challenge of "spicing-up" humdrum stories with compelling headlines.

When my career went on hold to have my two children, I freelanced as a copywriter. Having to dream up snappy advertisements and inspired articles on everything from hand-tools and staple guns, to womenswear and property sales was testing, but the wordplay came into its own.

It was while I was a young mum that my love for writing poetry developed. I used to keep a notebook in the kitchen drawer, jotting down thoughts as I cooked and cleaned, refining my ramblings on an Imperial typewriter. Friends would egg me on to publish my poems (some appeared in the Poetry Now series in the late 90s), but it has taken until now to publish this book. I hope you enjoy reading it as much as I have writing it.

Julie Anne Rudd

INDEX

1

ENIGMATIC WOMAN

Woman of many roles,
constantly changing,
new one for the day.
Domestic engineer,
just as at home at work,
child-minding her career.
Wife, mother and daughter,
caring and needing care.
Strong and independent,
weak and insecure.
Modern and classic,
simple and complex,
always and never the same.

2

CUTTING EDGE

Chaos rules supreme
for the working mum,
energy pushed to limit
keeping chaotic family
like the cutlery drawer,
functionally disordered.
Once meal is downed,
they're off to scatter
more disarray on her
neatly laid place settings.

Published in "In the Words of a Woman"
(Poetry Now) 1998

3

PRESSING ENGAGEMENT

My ironing board's a plane, a boat,
a train, I'm going globe-trotting,
travelling to places of great note,
really, I'm experience plotting.
Buttons, collars and cuffs,
around them I am riding.
How can I get the huff,
when I'm out astral gliding?
To America I'll fly Concorde,
sail the world in eighty days,
The Orient Express I'll board,
touring in, oh, so many ways!
Now my excursions have ended,
ironing done and energy spent,
travel is temporarily suspended,
till my next pressing engagement.

*(Featured in "The Hippies of Haggleby Hall",
Julie Anne Rudd 2017)*

4

BOSOM BUDDIES

Over shoulder, boulder holders,
bras both lacy and silky smooth,
stretch elastic for easy move.
Cups for small and larger measure,
just the job for work and leisure.
Underwire lifts and separates,
ensures our pair remain firm mates.
Removable pads, support for sags,
ranging in colours, styles and tags,
clips and fastenings, front or back,
adjustable straps balancing pack.
Cross my heart this is my size,
but looks all wrong, the label lies.
Finding the perfect fit for tits can
simply drive you out of your wits!

*(Featured in "The Hippies of Haggleby Hall",
Julie Anne Rudd 2017)*

5

PLAYING THE FIELD

Does man bowl maiden over in
the mating game? When she bats
her eyelids he'll aim to score,
but woman playing the field
has her boundaries. If he's
too fast he's on a sticky wicket
and could be stumped; too slow,
she might just duck and run.
But if he gets her out and
gives her a ball, it could be
a love-match. Winning her
over, that first kiss in the grass
has her in a spin and they're
heading for a life in clover.

6
LEAKY WEEKS

Is there anything worse
than the dreaded curse?
That time of the month
you're down in the dumps,
feeling ill, popping pills,
suffering pain that kills,
missing work, avoiding mates,
impossible to cope with dates,
staying home, aching head,
unhappy, snappy, best in bed,
feeling fat, stuffing cookies,
don't even want bit of nookie.
All because you give birth,
divine privilege your worth,
period piece of ovulation,
vital part of God's creation.

7

HORMONAL WASH DAY

Yesterday I was happy.
today I'm in the dumps.
How does a woman handle
those hormonal grumps?
I stick them in the washing,
like they are pairs of socks,
each day wear a fresh pair,
to keep me off the rocks.
When my head starts to spin
and I find it hard to cope,
I dial the rinse programme
and wring out all the soap.

8

PIPSQUEAK SHOPPING

Psyching up for weekly shop,
where shall it be today?
Have vouchers off for Tesco,
think I'll go Sainsbury's way.
Air miles in need of boost,
so onwards I am flying high
to do the dreaded deed or die!
Offers doing in my head:
'Buy one, get one free',
'Two for one' - I'm easily led,
'Double points all three'.
Trance-like I am queueing,
starving hungry, feet killing,
budget explodes with a bang.
Pay up, look cheerful n' willing!
Must try computer shopping;
With my mouse I can go at ease,
controlling spend and delivery,
my shopping it will be a breeze!

9
ALL OF A QUIVER

It's that time of year again,
Cupid's arrows are taking aim.
In your love make him believe,
wear your heart upon your sleeve.
Just stop beating about the bush,
all he needs is that little push.
The card shops you must brave,
there really is no time to save.
In choosing a message be bold,
here's your big chance he is told.
So, as lovers of the world unite,
allow your heart to join the flight
on this Valentine's red-letter day.
By firing off a message his way,
be it cryptic, funny, or straight,
it's the signal you want to date.
Today you are licensed to thrill
and Cupid's out to shoot at will!

10
DRIVING PASSION

Heart aching with long song,
miles melting to his door.
Deep sighs filling greeting,
lustful eyes seeking soul.
Strong arms, all embracing.
Heart racing for the moment.
Flesh brushing silky satin,
passion flowing undercovers,
firing deep within.
Feeling of arrival.
Fulfilled body sleeping.
Reality awakens,
clicking off car radio.

11

PRIZE BOOB

God made them to feed babies,
when Man was on all fours.
First buttocks attracted mates,
then boobs became the draw.
Now like fruit males compare;
melons, lemons, cherries,
and like the proverbial,
no two being the same.
But where did it all go wrong?
In the Garden of Eden,
where Eve, tempted by apple,
created Man's biggest boob.

12

HOOKED, LINE AND STINKER!

Lifelong promises pledged in minutes,
shiny gold rings seal newly-weds' kiss.
Nearest and dearest on photo parade,
wining, dining, toast to eternal bliss.
Hugs and farewells taking forever,
couple finally away in 'got-at' wheels;
slogans daubed, drink cans rattling.
Car wash ahead - given free deal!
What's that stink, something died?
It's kippers frying on the manifold
and marital bed's been "apple-pie-d"!
Still hungry for love, honeymooners?

13

LABOUR OF LOVE

Rumbling, grumbling,
tummy-gripping spasms,
tightening, frightening,
squeezing to release.
Panting, ranting,
puffing, pressing,
screaming, straining,
bursting to explode.
Hand-clasping, brow-
mopping, mumbling
masks supporting,
urging final effort.
Mighty pelvic pushing
exposes crowning glory,
liquid bundle expelling,
slithering to unload.
Protesting, wailing,
wondrous unwrapping,
brand new boy blazes
bloody victory trail.
Momentous occasion,
tears and elation,
joy of creation,
multiplication.

14

LOVESICK BLUES

Saturday is nookie night.
Supper served nice n' early,
offspring bribed to bed.
Dishwasher loaded sharpish.
Wine is working wonders.
Cuddles by cooker heating
to caressing under covers.
Earth is moving darling,
soaring up to heavens,
going into orbit, nearing
point of no return.
Banging getting louder.
"Mummy, gonna be sick!"
Rocket turning turtle,
diving rapidly downwards,
astronaut, anti-climaxed,
down bath plughole!

(Featured in in "The Hippies of Haggleby Hall", Julie Anne Rudd, 2017; "Game for A Laugh," Poetry Now 2000)

15

TROUBLE AFOOT

Son has started toddling,
cherished home's mobilised.
Drawers, cupboards opening,
doors to brave new world.
Plants, ornaments fragile,
strategically out of reach.
Explorer is on the loose,
trailing debris in his wake.
No peace for mummy,
fishing toothbrushes in loo,
or for daddy on computer,
as son flicks socket switch.
Junior's in double trouble,
plonked in prison cot.
Glass of wine outdoors,
temper control restores.
'Patio's drying nicely …
but what are those marks?
Oh, no, Trouble's
put foot in it - again!

16

JUNGLE LAW

Just as calm descends,
the kids wind us up again.
It's their turn to do dishes,
but they're waging war in
"jungle-biting" bedrooms.
Stepping into the breach
once more, spouse washes,
I dry, heads beating time
to heavy rock pounding
bedroom war dance above.
Job done, warriors call truce.
Peace restores, kids re-appear,
remind us pocket money due.
We teach them "give n' take"-
they do the taking and we give.
But revenge is, oh, so sweet,
one day it'll happen to them!

17

RAINBOW MAN

He picks me up when I am down,
makes me smile when I frown,
shows the way when I am lost,
gives his love counting no cost.
He cares for me when I am ill,
if I lose heart, gives me the will,
clears my mind when full of doubt,
teaches me what life's about.
He comforts me when I'm in pain,
makes the sun shine through rain.
My guiding light, my heavenly glow,
he's my multi-coloured rainbow.
Brilliant beam arching the sky,
I stand reflecting as to why
my pot of gold is at the end;
my rainbow man, my God-send.

For Bob

Published in "A Cry from The Soul"
(Poetry Now 2,000)

18
MASTER ESCAPE PLAN

Blond, blue-eyed bombshell
ready to explode. Six-foot,
six-pack, rated under five.
Train tracks tightening
crooked teeth in line.
Growth spurts downing
platefuls by the load.
Vocals deepening, looking
for a break. Hormones
erupting spots in clumps.
Females clawing to be a
willing mate. Mood swings
defying, sinking into sulks.
Home, school, pains in the
bum. Macho mind heading
for "master" escape plan.

19

GO-GETTER

Teens her prime time,
preening for a mate.
Horny males hovering,
desperate for a date.
Habitat the bathroom,
ages till she through.
Figure shaping up
to waist twenty-two.
Thigh-hugging skirts,
indecent any higher.
Hobby retail therapy,
fivers set on fire.
Make-up, nail varnish
belying tender years,
bubbling with energy,
laughter, tears n' fears.
Girlfriends a giggle,
endlessly they natter.
Boys, music, clothes,
all that really matter.
Can't and won't cook,
domestic chores no-nos.
Life's for chilling out,
where anything goes.

20

PREGNANT PAUSE

It's Mother's Day, hooray!
No cooking, no washing-up.
Breakfast in bed such luxury!
Family presents tea n' toast,
home-made cards and gifts.
Hugs and kisses all round.
Annual ritual done, they're
off to do their own thing.
Time to get back to earth;
dirty dishes await in sink,
washing to hang on line,
Sunday roast to prepare.
Little darlings squabbling.
And spouse? Gone to pub.
Mother's Day reminders
not to get pregnant again!

21
GRAND LADY

Granny turns off hearing aid
to little darlings' tantrums,
presents big bag of sweeties,
speeding milk teeth's demise.
She's always time for games,
in between television soaps,
loves cooking for everyone,
soggy sprouts her real forte.
She's great fun to be with,
when nothing's paining her,
laments all her yesterdays,
loses all hope for tomorrow.
She longs for us to visit her,
relieved when it's time to go,
lectures everyone on life,
finer details on who's died.
When family's together,
she loves us all to pieces!

22

MOTHER'S LAMENT

In your baby days
our lives were simple.
My hours were yours.
You were my everything.
Together we grew,
sharing the joys of
your little discoveries.
Now you are older,
I have to work,
my time taken up
helping pay our way.
How I wish life was
simple again; that we
could still have fun
without watching
the clock. Suddenly,
you are growing up,
learning for yourself,
and all I can do is stand
back, slowly let you go.
But wherever you are,
whatever you do, my
heart beats within you,
bonding inseparable.

23
DEADLY F-EMAIL

Gladys is an item,
Apple of his eye,
but what is on her menu?
It really makes me sigh!
Upstairs in the bedroom,
he's getting all keyed-up,
playing with her icons,
he's bound to come unstuck.
His little mouse just loves
him fingering her click,
their textual intercourse,
it really makes me sick!
He's losing all control,
going Google-eyed,
surfing the Internet to
another byte on the side.
Considering my actions,
I'll switch off the line.
I'll cause some ructions,
I will make him whine.
I'm going to pull the plug,
fill him with remorse.
I won't be a mug…
I'll file for divorce.

continued...

How spouse does cursor,
appearing with a frown,
Gladys has a deadly virus,
gone into total shutdown!

24

CHRISTMAS CRACK-UP

Nearly Christmas - have no fear!
Must keep going, it's getting near.
Hang the tinsel. Plan the meals.
Stock the freezer. Look for deals.
Cards unfinished, what a chore!
Keep on writing… still there's more.
Gifts conundrum, shop till I drop.
Bank balance red, stress over top.
House to clean, presents to wrap…
Oh, let's go away, scrap all that!

25
PAIN IN THE B...

Man and his piles, a very sore point.
No sitting down for poor spouse,
tidying his high-rises around house.
Yellowing letters, bills, till receipts,
he hangs on to them like grim death.
Hoarding must be in-built in male,
ever multiplying his paper empire.
Dump it or lump it, she must decide
between harmony and conflict.
A house-proud Jekyll and Hyde.

26

LOVE OVERGROWN

Summer-ripe raspberry sunset
lifts her heavy heart.
Warm still noise bids her to drive
down dark dappled lanes.
Woods are beckoning her return
to the place where limbs entwined.
A heady day in May when
magic cast its spell of passion.
Now tall bracken hides the place
where ecstasy lay in leaves.
As corn is cut sweet memories
fade with autumn's deadly kiss.

Published in "Closer Now to You"
(Poetry Now, 2,000)

27

BIG "FOUR-OH"!

Life begins at Forty,
they say I'm in my prime,
but now that I've got there
I'm on borrowed time.
Commiserate? Celebrate?
What is to be done, to mark
this dubious birthday?
Well, let's have some fun!
The party's all planned,
Please come, do not shirk,
we won't live forever
now that's a dead cert!

Sung to "Happy Birthday to You"

28
BURNT OUT

Dying embers of their love,
glinting brighter irony,
fading hot to cold.
Fireside feelings frozen,
locked in warp of time.
He remembers passion's flame,
warming hearth-rug's bare cheek;
salt-fresh romance, cliff-top high,
future hopes stretched out to sea.
She remembers family days,
time to stop, stare, and share.
But life moved on, ill-fortune
reducing eternity's dreams
to smouldering ashes.
He turned away, espied
a brighter world beyond.
He turned back.
She was still there,
but not her,
and he… another.

29

SONNET TO MOTHER

Shall I compare you to a fading sun,
shining on golden daffodils,
and when the day is nearly done,
casting shadows over grassy slopes?
Sometimes grey clouds may block
your golden rays, when there will be
a darker while, but every cloud
has a silver lining, they say;
then once again, people will smile.
Though you may dwindle and begin
to fade, you will still be free,
golden and roaming the skies,
lighting our lives, the happiness you made.
As your love remains the day will never die,
and as people look at your pretty face,
their hearts will be taken to a brighter place.

Becky Bowers, aged 11

30

GOING DOWN

Mini-skirts gave me a lift,
showing my shapely legs.
But with age marching on
my calves are losing tone,
my veins deepening blue.
Wearing short hems now
I'm mutton dressed as lamb.
Alas, my little black number
is off to the Ox Bros' rails;
the lift is going down to
the bargain basement.

31
GO-BETWEEN

Cathy has been duly engaged;
post-operative plumbing for spouse.
Their attachment has me enraged,
they're inseparable round the house.
She could easily drive him to drink,
but she's just a convenience I'd say.
As for drinking, well, he has to think;
a full glass, it would heavily weigh.
Temporarily she's his number one,
a wee help in helping him work.
But he moans she's really no fun,
if overloaded she will just shirk.
Cathy just goes with the flow,
and soon they will take her away.
They'll be no tears, tales of woe,
when he's free to pee again,
hooray!

32

GOLDEN GARDEN

How the years do hasten
since creation's priceless gift
you so selflessly bestowed
on us children, without fear.
With deepest hearts we thank
you for life's sacrifice so dear,
nurturing wondrous tiny buds
into precious heavenly blooms.
Family flowers flourish still
in your golden garden and
summer's sweetest scents will
linger forever in your souls.

(Parents' Golden Wedding anniversary)

33
PAPER MATES

Man's trouser pocket point
is inclined to take flight,
with some in their Forties,
it simply has to write.
With age creeping on,
hair greying, letting go,
it has this need to prove
how the ink can still flow.
On sheets between the lines
it pens its flush of youth,
proof he still has style.
But what is the real truth?
Wife, kids tossed aside,
with abandon of a loon,
written off in a flourish
to his signature tune.

34

STREET CREDIT

Look into my eyes
and take account.
I'm on the street,
seeking big amount.
You have the dough,
I'm making a pass,
just view my pupil
in peephole glass.
My name's Iris, I have
transaction to make;
seeing my balance,
from deposit I'll take.
Approving, you pay.
How looks can thrill,
making withdrawal at
"eye-dentity" cash till!

35

WYSIWYG

Appearing one by one,
snowflakes on the crown,
gently at first, then faster.
As blizzard heads in,
camouflage comes in bottle,
turning back tell-tale
signs on weathered face.
Age drifts ahead, melts
beneath ammonia n' peroxide.
Dyeing beauty's locks restored
to match box's lovely lady.
But as time takes its toll,
she'll be resorting to her
WYSIWYG!

36
BORN AGAIN WOMAN

Born again woman,
brainchild of the medics,
conceived in magical test
tube of eternal youth.
Hormonal balancing act
in new age of science.
Dwindling energy renews,
sluggish brain restores,
facial features freshen.
Confidence returns to
kick home new goals.
And it's all thanks to that
little pill, that sticky patch
they call HRT.

37

SOLE DESTROYING

They're breeding;
boots, wellies, shoes,
family footwear ready
to send you flying on
home assault course;
lurking under chairs,
lying in dark corners,
bushwhacking outside,
thanks to dippy dog!
Half pairs multiplying,
getting beyond a joke.
We need an authority,
for corrective training,
before we all end up like
our Lab … barking mad!

38

MIRACLE WORKER

Back man Bill will put me right.
I visit him with body tight.
He looks me up, looks me down.
I lie on couch, wearing a frown.
'Your line', he says, 'is out of true.
Now just relax, I'll deal with you.'
He gets to work, manipulates bones,
massages muscles, ignoring moans.
He can be gentle, heavy-handed,
reaching pain not always candid.
His iron hand in velvet glove
adjusts my vertebrae with love.
I want to laugh, want to cry,
but soothing music gets me by.
Up in the clouds I float away,
won't come back till another day.
Then, carefully does it, up I get,
feeling better – that's a sure bet!
When Bill puts his back into mine,
his miracle touch is simply divine!

39
DOG'S BODY

Dusting the house drives me mad,
makes me sneeze, must be bad.
Hoovering dog's hairs, a pet hate;
ears ring, back hurts, arms ache.
Bedrooms, bathroom, staircase,
lounge, this time I'm going apace.
Shades, skirtings, mirrors, doors,
flick them all, then wash floors.
So much to do, never beat it yet,
must stay on top, not get upset.
Am pooped when cleaning done,
but full of pride the battle's won!
Family back, pooch trailing mess.
No worry, dogsbody's here, I guess.

40
HANGING LOOSE

It's time for a holiday,
I keep making blunders.
Let's book a package,
it will work wonders.
A change of scene;
we need a break away.
You want golf, TV bars,
but let me have a say.
Walking, sight-seeing,
I love my days out.
But you? Sun-bathing,
just lazing till I shout.
I hate fast-food joints,
clubbing, late nights.
You loathe shopping,
touring all the sights.
Let's go with own mates,
loosen our wedding ties;
two weeks in agreement,
the perfect compromise.

41
DOUBLE LIFE

She cooks for him,
cleans for him,
sews his socks.
She waits on him,
washes for him,
does the shop.

She dresses for him,
makes-up for him,
listens to his woes.
She entertains him,
performs for him
between bedclothes.

Two women in his life,
two worlds in his life,
two people are he.
Bewitched his life,
Betwixt his life,
which of him is true?

42

SETTLING OLD SCORES

Humid courtroom judge
directs settlement outside.
Aptly-sited war memorial
couple's bargaining scene.
She in red corner sits atop
low wall, dabbing eyes.
He, in blue, stands stony-
faced, foot fidgeting gravel.
Barrister calculates rapid
arithmetic; solicitor bat n'
balls hard to bend sums.
Church clock counts agony
minutes to compromise;
suiting neither to suit both.
Inside, judge convivially
rubber-stamps agreement.
Couple, relieved, extend
handshake truce. Silver
partnership evaporates,
singular paths distancing,
going opposite ways.

43
TOP MANAGEMENT

One of life's biggest bores,
taking control of my hair.
If I don't style when wet,
it curls and goes frizzy.
If I just comb and leave it,
I'll look like a scarecrow.
When I blow dry with care,
the weather will wreck it.
I've tried many a new look,
but the long 'n short of it,
I always resort to old one.
On bad hair days I stuff it
underneath a scarf or hat.
But on the rare occasions
when it just falls into place,
I feel like a million dollars,
ready to take on the world!

44

UNDERCOVER AGENTS

Our body protectors,
keeping us safe at night.
A reassuring presence,
dispelling bad dreams.
Our loyal guardians,
warding off all fears.
Faithful companions,
during darkest hours.
Our undercover allies,
clothing naked truth.
Buttoned and tucked,
we're armed and ready
to leg it to land of Nod.
Our perfect partners;
when sleeping alone
we girls just love
our trusty "jim-jams"!

45
FITTING REUNION

You're back in my life,
a missing piece of jigsaw,
fallen out of its box,
into a dark drawer.
You were always there,
outlined in the picture,
my life taking shape
with fitting and fixture.
Thought you'd gone forever,
accepted that little space.
You were a cut-out memory
of a former time and place.
A puzzle starts at nothing,
blank emptiness before me,
scattered senseless shapes
needing patient harmony.
But, unlike life's picture,
I know a puzzle's form,
and can fit back together
lost pieces that are found.
And now you are back,
part of a perfect whole,
let us keep together,
till God rests our souls.

46

NAILING YOUR CATCH

Your nails need to be cherished.
Neatly-manicured and polished,
colour-matching eyes and lips,
girl power at your fingertips,
giving that extra dimension,
reaching out for his attention.
Be painstaking when painting,
letting dry and careful dressing,
then you're ready for impressing.
Luring the one you want to land,
he'll be eating out of your hand.

47
FIT FOR A QUEEN

Man on ladder upside down,
wind ripples canopy fringe,
ceiling crack fastens eyes.
Whirring sound in my head,
mind drifts to special place;
turtle beach of blissful calm.
Wintery blast flaps picture,
window closes to the world.
Chair captive begs for release
in a silent scream … not yet!
Jaw endures invasion's ache;
losing nerve in masked pain,
soon I'll be wearing a crown,
with a smile fit for a queen.

48
TICKLED PINK

It all started when I was a baby;
my knits from gran, blankets maybe.
As I grew it was party dresses and toys,
cherished possessions of girls, not boys.
Over the years it became my first love,
ever present from handbag to glove.
It was, still is, my number one choice,
my persona, my image, inner voice.
Now, as I disgracefully grow old,
it's part of me in evidence bold;
my phone, laptop, my trainers too,
are not in colour of baby boy blue,
but in the shade of a little Miss,
as is my sparkly pen drafting this.

49
SUPERMAN

He travels the world for a living,
the miles tend to be unforgiving,
but he returns home full of zest,
to do new tasks in marital nest.
He's our rock as we grow older,
a fit young man so much bolder,
always there in times of need,
his only reward a slap-up feed.
A helping hand, moral support,
assisting us with kind thought.
In difficulty he'll devise a plan,
solve the problem best he can.
He'll not stop till it's overcome.
My Superman, my dearest son.

50
COMING UP ROSES

You may have seen it all before,
looking back, divorce quite raw.
Then someone new comes along,
makes you feel loved and strong.
Your fingers burnt once, look out,
that voice in your head will shout.
Take your time. What's the hurry?
Be careful of infatuation's flurry!
If he loves you much as he says,
he will be happy to bide his days.
"Once bitten twice shy" they say,
so, live it up while you can today.
If you have a home of your own,
it's your sanctuary to rule alone.
Enjoy both worlds while you can,
before a "Yes" to your new man.
Play it cool, just in case it sours.
Smell roses before bridal flowers.

51

MATERIAL HEALTH

'Good morning new day!'
I have lived another night
to greet you at my window
in the gently growing light.
As the sun lifts its smiley face
I welcome you into my sight,
to fulfil longed-for hopes,
achieve ambition's height;
a big house in the country,
a new washing machine,
a car to replace old banger,
that holiday of my dream.
But as the fresh day dawns,
all that really matters to me
is a letter in the post to say,
"Test results Cancer free".

52

DEAD BEAT

My faithful culinary mate
is in a parlous state,
its slicers, whisks and blades
are starting to misbehave.
When on it wobbles n' shakes,
making meringues and cakes.
The longer it has to beat,
the motor will overheat.
Its plastic stand and stay
are close to giving way.
My 40-year-old wedding gift
gave my cuisine such a lift,
aided many a food process,
helped me be a good hostess.
Now worn out, beyond its best,
it's what you call "going west",
but leaving my equipment mix,
its new model is a quicker fix!

53
MY BEST FRIEND

She's my best friend and I love her tons,
She lives away, but sometimes comes.
We'll go swimming, sightseeing, walking,
share cups of tea, spending hours talking.
Her life's full on when she gets cracking,
and her phone calls they can be lacking,
but she's in regular touch on WhatsApp,
multi-tasking, still managing to chat.
She is pretty, witty, cute and clever,
faces challenge with great endeavour.
On life's rich path she loves to travel,
problems in her way she'll just unravel.
When troubled we help each other by,
though we don't always see eye to eye.
At times she drives me round the bend,
but I will love her always because
she's my daughter, my best friend!

54

LADY IN DE-STRESS

Now, first things first
and second, second,
just where do I begin?
With thirds and fourths
mounting priorities,
my day is caving in!
Sit down, breathe deep,
counting one to twenty,
switch off and do re-set.
Hey presto, I'm all ready
now to do one at a time,
order sifting, no sweat!
I'm getting more done,
keeping my cool - but
then it happens again!
The list keeps growing,
it's self-perpetuating,
think I'm going insane!
So I, multi-tasking, sit
down, breathe deeply,
counting one to twenty,
this stress I will master!

55
THANKS BE TO MUM

Thank you my most special mum,
you are simply one of the best.
As mother, wife and grandmother
you are heads above the rest.
Thank you for your listening ear,
a shoulder for me to cry on,
there to advise, not patronise,
someone I can totally rely on.

Thank you for a happy childhood,
my beloved sister, my playmate,
those wonderful family memories,
shaping we young adults in wait.
Thank you for a loving, safe home,
for your nurturing over the years,
my rock, mentally and spiritually,
helping me overcome all my fears.

Thank you for always being there
in times of difficulty and illness.
My trouble sharer, loyal carer,
bringing your calm and stillness.
Thank you for teaching me ABC,
encouraging with gentle ways,

continued...

supporting me through GCEs to
achieve my goals in working days.

Thank you for a stable upbringing,
happy home and devotion to Dad,
a blueprint for our family values,
for which we are eternally glad.
Thank you for making me as I am,
your pillar of strength in my soul.
Thank you for LIFE, mother dear,
for helping me to become whole.

56
THIN END OF THE WEDGE

Just one more chocolate
and that is it; I'll not touch
another till I lose a stone.
No more munching biscuits,
polishing off kids' leftovers,
nibbles in front of the tele.
Wardrobe's full of clothes
bursting at the seams.
Me midriff's gone adrift,
behind's on sit-down strike.
Must join Weight Watchers,
Keep Fit, get to the gym …
next week. There's a new
me just 'lying in weight' -
with a fat chance of success.

57

HARD-STRETCHED

On my mat I'm focused pelvic floor,
scooping up abs, strengthening core.
Teacher's voice, soft and soothing,
encourages us with gentle moving
to calming music, up and down,
stretching, relaxing in the round.
But, instead of body limbering up,
muscles tighten, 'Help, I'm stuck!'
A guiding hand shows the way,
I do as instructed without delay.
As class is full must keep in sync,
or bash neighbour, I have to think.
Now it's beans can lifts, oh no,
hold them tight or break me toe!
Next pull stretchy band to limit,
don't let go - or rebound with it!
Any which way I must stay loose,
keep in control or what's the use?
An hour and a bit's enough for me,
but without doubt I'm feeling free.
At last it's time to snuggle and rest
beneath blanket - well, did my best.
Yogalates keeps us fit, makes us laugh
- it's worth the aches in the aftermath.

58
TIME FOR HOME

See heavenly sky, my love,
no clouds can fill.
God's garden rich, my love,
no labour to will.

His home awaits, my love,
no pressures or strings,
to bring you rest, my love,
all favourite things.

Success, failure, my love,
no place for them here,
be happy, at peace, my love,
without any fear.

No time to age, my love,
years bring no ill health,
no pain or sorrow, my love,
perfection your wealth.

A child you are, my love,
God loves you dear,
no harm to hurt, my love,
He is always here.

continued…

Your toil is done, my love,
no demands on your time.
Drift in pure bliss, my love,
everything is just fine.

(In memory of Bob)

59
CHILD'S PLAY

You're going back, a child again,
to the times you had left behind,
aged three, sitting on warm knee,
book of nursery rhymes to read.
Tired tears drying, fears calming,
so, let's be off to the park for a lark,
riding roundabout, swings and slide,
shaking insides, feel dizzy and sick.
Going back, questions: 'What's dat?'
'Why?' 'Can 'ave ice-cream?' A treat!
At home after drink you're ready to
sink into chair, but you must take
magic carpet ride to faraway isle,
then boat sailing high seas to hunt
lost treasure. No time for leisure.
'Quick, run, hide behind settee, the
monsters are coming to get you!'
'We must flee - too late! Keep down,
don't breathe! Phew, they've gone'.
Tummy's rumbling, stop grumbling,
share your lunch with Talky Ted,
Molly Dolly and their little friends!
Let's have a snooze, resting on floor;
but soon sun floods in through door,

continued…

So out you must pop, race to the fence,
run slowly, you *simply* have to lose!

After hour guarding castle, killing giant,
battling monster, you're too exhausted
for any more adventure, so time for TV,
eating your tea before splash in the bath.
'A bedtime story, please, please', eyes
prised open not to sleep. Time to turn
off light, 'Night-night'. Kissing cheek,
you must leave your little friend now;
your child's child, and when to your
bed you must wend, you will dream
of those days long ago, when you
were a child wearing out Grandma!

60
BACK AND FORWARD

Age is just a number,
you begin losing count,
but does it really matter
forgetting right amount?
Accept aches and pains,
your body on the wane,
balance rest and play,
getting old is not a game.
Keep fit, eat healthily,
be mindful of old adage,
"Use it, or lose it"- but do
your emotional baggage!
Be a "new-age" pensioner,
staying young at heart,
no need for over-doing it,
pacing yourself is smart.
If you're doing all of these,
but something still you lack,
spread love and help others;
it's all about putting back -
and memories left behind.

6 1
JOURNEY THROUGH LIFE

Whispers,
whispers so silent,
are now getting louder.
Footsteps so soft,
are now getting heavier.
Thick darkness, getting lighter.
Tense fingers,
clasping tighter.
Long tunnel,
getting shorter.
Eternal life,
coming closer every day.

Becky Bowers
("Poetry Now South East" 1998)

Retired journalist Julie Anne Rudd spent most of her working life newspaper reporting and sub-editing in London, Surrey, Sussex and Kent, although her poetry writing days began at home as a young mum, when she had a number of her verses published in the popular Poetry Now series of the Nineties. Now a published author living in Devon, she still enjoys penning poems on various subjects and particularly enjoys those for women.

Some of her poetry features in her debut novel of 2017, a comedy mystery, "The Hippies of Haggleby Hall" (available from Amazon Books) and there will be more in her sequel, "The Race is On," which she is presently writing. Julie Anne aims to publish her poetry on other subjects later.

If you have enjoyed reading these poems you are welcome to post a review either on Amazon, Goodreads or on Julie Anne's Facebook page, thank you.

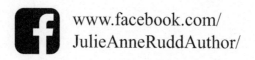 www.facebook.com/
JulieAnneRuddAuthor/

Printed in Great Britain
by Amazon